MW01243963

CAPITALISM WIIFM

It's the Key to Your Future

Ken West

Better Grip Publishing

ISBN-13: 978-0-9825777-3-8

Cover photo by Johannes Plenio on Unsplash
Cover design by: Art Painter
Library of Congress Control Number: 2018675309
Printed in the United States of America

To Ayn Rand, who was the inspiration for this book.

"Capitalism was the only system in history where wealth was not acquired by looting, but by production, not by force, but by trade, the only system that stood for man's right to his own mind, to his work, to his life, to his happiness, to himself."

AYN RAND

CONTENTS

PREFACE

When I wrote this book, I was a young man, having spent a considerable amount of time researching everything I could find about the nature of capitalism.

My goal was to define what capitalism meant to me and share what I found out.

Instead, I stuffed my manuscript into a drawer and left it there for years.

I rediscovered it under a pile of other papers and then reread it.

The younger version of me hadn't had the confidence to publish it.

But the older version of myself was finally ready to send it out into the world.

If it helps you understand, appreciate, defend, and enjoy capitalism (as it has for me), then I will achieve my purpose.

I hope you benefit from reading about the many facets of the marvelous system called capitalism.

INTRODUCTION

Photo by Nirzar Pangarkar on Unsplash

Capitalism is an economic, social, and political system built upon individual initiative.

It is a mistake to think of capitalism as a collective, macro-economic chess game where big business, big labor, and big government make all the moves. Viewing it this way obscures its true nature.

To understand, appreciate, and profit from capitalism, you need to see it from the individual's vantage point, especially from your own life.

First and foremost, capitalism is a system of organized individualism.

Individuals are the operative players. And when groups of individuals join voluntarily to form businesses and corporations, it is individuals who choose whether to do so or not.

Capitalism is the economic system of the individual.

Learning about capitalism begins with you. The first question you might ask is, "What's in it for me?" The answer may be more than you realize.

Take a dream you may have of a better life. Do you believe it is possible? Why do you think it is or is not?

Capitalism is a system that encourages possibilities. Under capitalism, anything is possible because its motive power is the stuff life is made of — self-interest and the quest for happiness.

How does one achieve happiness? Is it easy? The answer is in the phrase "personal struggle."

Nothing is given to us but our present circumstances.

The raw material of your success comes from your motivation to succeed. You struggle and grapple with life to get what you desire and dream about.

In a capitalist social system, you have the freedom to do this rationally and peacefully.

It's time to stop taking capitalism for granted. Let's explore its many facets.

The purpose of this book is to help you discover what's in it for you.

Then you can profit from it as you realize what a miraculous system it is.

You can learn to use it.

PRIVATE PURPOSES

Photo by Elizabeth Kay on Unsplash

Capitalism does not have an all-inclusive, top-down purpose.

It has no direct purpose of its own.

Under it, you seek your happiness in life, whatever that may be. You follow your purpose. Capitalism ensures *freedom of purpose*.

If you are an adherent of a religion or new philosophy, your purpose reflects your beliefs.

If you seek to get rich, your purpose may be to start a business and make money.

Suppose you march to the beat of a different drummer. In that case, capitalism leaves you free to pursue your ideas — freedom to seek the presidency or become a hermit.

Under top-down systems (communist, socialist, fascist), an all-encompassing state purpose is forced on the society.

Capitalism, on the other hand, does not prescribe any specific, all-inclusive purpose.

It leaves it up to you to decide what you will live your life for and what goals you will pursue (as long as you respect others' rights to do the same).

Capitalism doesn't tell you how to live. It lets you live your life as you see fit.

Think of capitalism as an organic process for living that allows every person to decide how to spend their lives.

If you are looking for total security — look elsewhere; capitalism cannot guarantee it.

The streets are not paved with gold — but they are paved. You can travel in any direction you choose.

The essence of capitalism is the *empowerment of private purpose.*

You decide your purpose, no one else.

CHOICES

Photo by Cenk Batuhan Özaltun on Unsplash

Freedom is the easiest thing in thing in the world to take for granted until you lose it. It is also the most demanding way of life because everything becomes a choice.

The first choice you are confronted with in a capitalist country is what to do with your freedom, which leads to many specific choices:

- What will make you happy?
- What shall you do to earn your living?
- What is most important to you?
- Where will you work?
- Who will buy your labor, your product, your service, or even your business?
- Should you work for yourself as an entrepreneur or as an employee for a company of your choice?

- Who would you like to serve, not as a "selfless" altruist duty, but as your client, customer, employer, or target audience?
- What career or profession do you choose to pursue?

To live with the freedom of a capitalist society, you take responsibility for your own life and the choices you make. It is your responsibility.

Personal choice is what it's about.

You choose your purpose, goals, methods, means, actions, products, and services. Everything is a choice. If you make enough right choices and carry them out, you will eventually be successful, although success can never be guaranteed.

In essence, capitalism is the freedom to choose your goals, fulfill them by actions, and own the results — so long as you do not infringe on the rights of others to do the same.

Personal choice is the pivot of our economy. For most modern businesses, the more options you give your customers, the more opportunities you will have to grow and succeed.

Later, in this book, we will spend time talking about capitalism's enemies. The freedom of choice we have as producers and consumers is one thing that critics of capitalism despise the most. They don't believe in unlimited freedom of choice. Instead, they want to impose their view of "the good" on the rest of us.

The writer, Eric Hoffer, defined such a person as "a self-appointed soul engineer who sees it as his sacred duty to operate on mankind with an ax."
Capitalism is intolerable to them precisely because it does not dictate a top-down, allegedly altruistic purpose.

Altruism is the belief that you should live *primarily* — first and foremost — for the benefit of others. (The popular conception of altruism as benevolence to others is not its actual meaning.) Altruism allows every kind of evil so long as it is allegedly "for the good of others" regardless of the consequences. For a full discussion of the real meaning and results of altruism, read Ayn Rand's writings. Start with her extraordinary novel, *Atlas Shrugged.*

You can make a fundamental choice to disagree with your government, or your peers, or the status quo. Capitalism protects the right to disagree. As Ayn Rand has said, "the right to agree is never a problem in any society — rather it is the right to disagree that is crucial."

When an entrepreneur disagrees, they do so by creating new methods, products, or services. Usually, these are scoffed at until they succeed.

When a writer or speaker disagrees with some aspect of government policy or modern life, they usually go against the current trend of thought and beliefs.

In both cases, capitalism, because it does not have an all-inclusive state purpose other than ensuring freedom itself, allows these entrepreneurs or social critics the freedom of action necessary to carry out their plans.

It has nothing to say to them other than pursue your purpose while respecting others' rights.

It is private property that allows them to do this. In a society that protects private property, one can usually find the physical means and support to accomplish goals.

Let's consider the case of social critics.

With socialism, many sources of funding and support are not possible. The government is either the sole employer and distributor of goods and services or the de facto regulator of all economic activity.

Under such a system, everything is a political decision. There are little or no private sources of funding.

Imagine that you have just come up with a devastating attack on a present government leader, or you have developed a new philosophy that is critical of the current system of government. You have ample evidence and plenty of intellectual ammunition to wage your campaign.

How would you proceed from here?

In a socialist or communist state, you would have to convince the state-controlled publishers to print your thesis or produce your product.

Of course, they would tell you that you must get permission from the commissar of political opinion, a committee of "your peers," and that you must belong to the writer's union. Since your material is critical of those in power, you would not get a bureaucrat to go along with you.

Although you are free to attempt those things in our mixed-economy, regulatory roadblocks, entrenched political forces, social media "fact-checkers," and a host of other restraints can deflect your every move.

Free speech, you soon find out, requires the ability to translate your ideas into written or physical form and physically distribute your message unchecked by government bureaucrats.

Today, of course, we have social media. Yet those "fact-checkers" are hard at work trying to weed out any contrary opinions that go against the "accepted" truth.

Under a capitalist system, the government cannot prevent you from obtaining what you need to spread your message, so long as you get it lawfully. You are free to obtain the materials or convince some publisher or publication to take a chance on your message.

Karl Marx got his message published and printed in a capitalist country — and so did Ayn Rand. In a capitalist society, you fight bad ideas with better ones.

And those ideas can be converted into physical form and take on a life of their own.

Ideas need physical expression — private property. Our next chapter deals with the means used to translate dreams into reality in a capitalist society.

MEANS

Photo by Minh Pham on Unsplash

To carry out any goal or plan, we need certain materials.

If you are an artist, you would need canvas, paints, an easel, a place to paint, many other items, and time to carry on your activity. This material or the money needed to purchase it is called your capital.

Capital is the money or material needed to produce or accomplish any productive activity. It is the lifeblood of production. Human ability is the heart and soul.

Capitalism allows individuals to accumulate capital and thus the physical power and tools to accomplish goals. Socialist or communist societies either severely limit one's ability to accumulate capital or outlaw it. (Think of Cuba and North Korea.)

This chapter is about the physical means necessary to produce any good or service. As with our hypothetical example about social critics in the last chapter, capitalism protects the right to disagree.

In a very fundamental sense, all production is disagreement with the status quo. Human beings can change their environment via production, using nature's powers and re-channeling them to suit our purposes.

All products, services, and ideas aim at some change or betterment in the status quo. A capitalist system is forward-looking and growth-oriented. (Environmentalists attack capitalism for changing nature's status quo.)

The first of the means at your disposal is your mind. The human brain is a vastly complex biological computer that can change the world — when backed up by the human will.
Human ability is the channeling of your brainpower into physical action.

Capital is the money, material, and tools needed to power your physical and mental efforts and give your ideas form. In essence, you are converting thoughts and energy into matter — products, services, or works of art.

You can obtain capital from many sources in a capitalist social system. You may save what you can from your earnings and borrow what you need from many sources — from your parents, friends, banks, organizations, investors, or venture capitalists.

To get people to lend you money and invest in your ideas, you must convince them that it makes sense and profit them. To be successful, you must appeal to their self-interest.
Capitalism does not allow force — only persuasion.

Capitalist society has myriad independent sources of support. There are no guarantees, but you can succeed. Capitalism is a system of possibilities. You would not be able to get your new product or service off the drawing board in a socialist system with its top-down prescribed goals.

You can also hire others to help you achieve your goals. You hire their labor, which is their skills, brainpower, or physical strength, to help with your purpose. You also hire those with a series of hard to define skills, but the result is someone who can get the job done efficiently.

When someone works for you, they do so only if they perceive it as beneficial to them in some way — that it suits their own purpose in life.

Sometimes it is merely the money you offer, but it is often the chance to do work that they enjoy.

Capitalism allows personal mobility to move to where the work is and freedom to specialize in the work that best suits you. You can work for others directly or as independent contractors.

In any event, there are never total guarantees of ultimate security. There is no such thing as total security.

As I will state later in this book — governments that attempt to offer security to their citizens extract a high price in terms of personal liberty. And in terms of reality, the price is eventual stagnation and decay.

You and I *are* the economy. Our choices and actions determine the health and vitality of "society."

Critics of capitalism complain that it values private property and profit above human beings. What these critics do not mention is that private property and profit are natural extensions of man.

Property and profit are what human beings need to convert their dreams into reality. It is also their result and reward for a successful effort.

Private property is the fruit of labor, both physical and mental.

When a farmer changes unproductive land into a successful farm, his labor and intelligence have accomplished that feat. Luck and the weather can play havoc in the short term, but in the long term, it is hard work — both physical and mental — that pays off.

Labor in this context is not the mere physical exertion of the muscles but also the thinking and planning that went into it.

Intelligence, foresight, planning, and hard work are the cornerstones of property.

In the case of a plot of land, house, factory, or even a book — your foresight, intelligence, ability, labor, etc., went into your product.

You earned the right to call it your own. You paid for it with your thought, labor, or hard-earned money — which represents stored energy — ready to use when needed.

When you own something, be it a car, a building, an artwork, or anything, you have the right to decide what to do with it or how to dispose of it.

There is a contest going on today between two philosophical camps. The first camp believes that everything is a collective, beehive, or anthill where you are a small unit in a grand design chosen by your leaders.

The second camp believes that you are an end in yourself and have the right and obligation to choose your purpose in life and own your rewards or losses accordingly.

ACTION

Photo by Pedro Santos on Unsplash

With Capitalism you are an active agent of change — if you think for yourself and have the courage of your convictions.

As an active agent of change, you choose your goals, seek out the means to accomplish them, and finally, take action.

The marketplace is the place where you act. Therefore, you need to know the market's reality — its movers, shakers, and connectors.

You accomplish your goals by taking intelligent, rational actions, utilizing your unique abilities and skills. Human ability is the heart and soul of production and Capitalism.

When you produce anything, you take possibilities and convert them by hard work, mixed with intelligence and discipline, into actualities. That is what production is all about.

Business is the rational control of production. It is the modern means of survival. Yet, Barbarians hate it for its rationality and for the fact that it requires an adult way of coping with reality. It requires one to face facts.

Many of us are sometimes guilty of the child-like wish that things would become true just by wishing them to be true and not having to work hard and smart.

When pursued by adults, this child-like wish is responsible for much of the violence, crime, and pain in the world. Criminals are the worst practitioners of this policy. So are some politicians.

Everything must be paid for by effort, then trading our skills and products in the marketplace. A criminal or a looter is an adult with a child-like mentality who does not know how or does not want to obtain values by intelligent effort while not violating individual rights. In other words, they want something for nothing.

What business (and Capitalism) does is allow the child within us to fulfill our dreams via reason, foresight, and hard work. The child's value is to dream; the adult's value is to convert dreams into reality by productive work. The child and the adult are in all of us. We need to keep them in harmony, for they create the greatness of life.

In the long run, you get what you create. The capitalist golden rule is "you get what you produce and create," which also includes the *results* created by your actions.

Business is the modern way to carry on production and exchange.

It is a productive activity. One seeks to exchange created products for money. To do this, one produces a product that people are willing to buy. One creates something of value to exchange for something else of value (money or barter).

No matter what your occupation — whether you are a coal miner, an artist, a philosopher, or all three — to succeed, you must *maximize your opportunities for making exchanges*. (This is one reason while networking and other means of connecting with others is so important.)

You do this by producing the best work you can and then becoming a good businessperson. You market and sell your product (and labor).

Business is the formalized methods that help you to sell your wares and make money. This, in turn, allows you to survive and prosper in the world.

Is it easy to succeed in the business of living? No. It is a struggle and an adventure that needs your long-term commitment to yourself and your ideas.

Production is a struggle against time. Labor-saving devices are *time-saving* devices. If you act wisely, rationally, and take some well-calculated risks, your chances for success are good.

Risk and insecurity go hand in hand. You must be prepared to make mistakes and take occasional losses.

But when you know your options and take intelligent risks, your potential to succeed in a capitalist system is high.

When you do so, you are giving up present security for future benefit. It is what life demands of us if we want to succeed. All government, business, or individuals' attempts to create absolute security, instead create flannel straitjackets that kill ambition and excitement.

The rules of the game: Take your ideas seriously. Trust yourself. Take Action.

How many people do you know who are afraid to give up their

present job? They hate it, but they're scared to give up their salary and benefits. It is a common problem.

But those who dare to trek out on their own and take risks and disagree with conventional wisdom have succeeded with surprising regularity. It is not easy. You must pay your dues to life. Many fail. But even in failing, they realize that they have become active agents of change in the world.

Now is the time to get out into that world.

PUBLIC PERFORMANCES

Photo by Jordan on Unsplash

Now you come with your purpose and goals into the world of other private objectives and goals. In a capitalist society, you are free to deal with others on a strictly voluntary basis.

If your purpose and goals mesh with mine, we may join for a moment or a lifetime.

Capitalism is a system of competition and cooperation.

We compete in buying and selling goods and services.

But we also cooperate in organizations and more fundamentally by adhering to capitalist society's essential ground rules: no one may initiate physical force against another or coerce them or cheat them.

Capitalism is a civilized means to trade the products of our labor without resorting to barbarism and conquest. It is the moral thing to do.

When we "*make* money" it means we have created a product or service that others are willing to pay for because it benefits their life in some way.

You are not allowed to *take* money, which is stealing. Instead, you *make* money. You *make* it by hard work and intelligence.

You offer people something of value to them.

You enter the public world with your product, trying to find and convince others that it will benefit them.

What allows you to do this peacefully is a base of law and order that any society needs to survive.

In a capitalist society, this base of law has as its purpose the protection of individual rights. It facilitates and enhances freedom.

In a dictatorship, law and order are used for the opposite purpose — to keep people in subjugation. And, in a mixed economy, it is partial subjugation.

The government in an actual capitalist society protects individual rights.

Each individual is free to pursue their own private purposes as long as they do not violate others' same rights.

Government is the agency that provides a unique service — the protection of the rights of all to take actions necessary for our survival as human beings.

Now, let us focus on the arena where we peacefully trade our products, ideas, and services.

THE MARKET

Photo by Collie Coburn on Unsplash

Consider Capitalism as organized individualism.

The market is the arena in which you trade or exchange your products for the money or products of others. It not only feeds us but also makes life much more exciting and enjoyable.

The market, which encompasses the whole world, is where you make voluntary deals and agreements to exchange your ideas, products, or labor.

Therefore, you need to be out there or have your representatives out there in whatever segment of your market.

Suppose you are trying to sell your invention, or artwork, or a philosophical treatise. In that case, you need to show potential buyers or readers that your product exists and benefits their life somehow.

If you're selling to a business, you must show potential buyers or investors that it will make them money — a lot of it!

The first way you do this is to show it off. Let them see it. Let them know about it.
Today, we have the Internet.

Your invention might end up being displayed in a hardware store or on Amazon.com.

Your artwork may appear in a retail art gallery and an online equivalent.

Your philosophical treatise could be in a bookstore, on the Internet, or both,

Is this easy to accomplish? No, it may take negotiation, contracts, persistence, faith in yourself, and your work.

You've got to make sure that enough of the right people see your product.

You maximize your opportunities for making exchanges.

The more that you expose your ego to the world, the more successful you can become.

But there's a price.

You deal with the fact that some will not like you or your products — and say so loudly and clearly.

Some will be indifferent.

Yet, those that matter will like you and buy your products — whether those products be bars of soap, music, works of art, novels, philosophical treatises, or any product or service produced.

If you are a writer, inventor, or artist, this means getting your work finished and into the world in as many places and hands as possible.

It means that many people will not like your work and say so.

It also means that many will like it, say so, and buy it.

It is a matter of time, persistence, and work.

Many find it difficult: They are afraid of being rejected, hurt, ignored, or humiliated.

We all must overcome that fear if we want to see our product survive and become successful.

You must be selfish enough to want the best for yourself and be willing to work for it.

If you allow yourself to be a loser mentally, you will not have the strength to carry your project to its completion.

As the writer Dorothea Brand wrote in her classic book Wake Up and Live, you must "act as if it is impossible to fail."

When you have a temporary failure, welcome it as proof you are trying and doing something.

Successful people fail more than unsuccessful people, but they pick themselves up and go from where they are.

They learn, not taking temporary failure personally. Their ego stays intact.

The time for doubts is over.

The time to act is now and throughout the rest of your life.

It is all you have.

Nothing else will do.

Let's summarize:

Potential customers must be convinced that your product, service, or idea will benefit them.

In the case of an artwork — the convincing is a confrontation with your work of art.

With an invention or a philosophical treatise, they may need to see how the features benefit them.

Negotiation, marketing, advertising, promotion, persuasion, and salesmanship come into the equation.

You must passionately believe in your product and be willing to stake your reputation on it.

There are no bureaucrats to hide behind.

You are your first and best salesman and promoter.

The thing about the market that makes it unique is its unpredictability.

Economists have identified the economic principles at work. Yet, no one can predict the cross-fertilization of ideas and the chance encounters of individuals that result in an entirely new product or service, or industry.

This is why cities are centers of creativity and productivity generators.

It is nearly impossible to plan for or arrange all the interactions of buyers and sellers and inventors and thinkers in the marketplace before these interactions happen.

This is one reason why central planning of the economy does not work.

It attempts to control the economy, which means managing

human interactions. Governments create regulations and rules that effectively put people and their ideas into a planning strait-jacket.

All human progress has resulted from individuals free enough and brave enough to pursue their unique ideas and talents to bring them to fruition.

Thinking is an individual process.

Those who believe central planning works think that individuals should comply and work for top-down goals under compulsion.

Men and women must be free to openly pursue their thoughts and bring their ideas to the marketplace.

What a free marketplace leads to and engenders is an open, liberal society.

Interestingly, both present-day liberals and many conservatives seem to resent our society's complete openness if it conflicts with their views.

A capitalist society is one of a wide diversity in ideas and prod-ucts (and people).

It allows challenges to be made to the system itself that socialist, fascist, or communist systems cannot tolerate.

In the final analysis, all values enter the capitalist marketplace where they must prove themselves.

Capitalism could be said to be the freedom to exchange values.

Our next chapter is all about Values.

VALUES

Photo by Tom Ezzatkhah on Unsplash

Capitalism empowers and protects the voluntary exchange of values.

But what are values?

Critics of capitalism have long scorned that rock stars or professional athletes make more money than concert pianists or cancer researchers. Or that people spend more money on hamburgers than cancer research.

One of the central confusions of the term "value" is in what sense or context it is being used.

Critics of the system use the term "value" to mean the intrinsic worth of a product, service, work of art, or idea. They are talking about some inner value.

They can claim that a particular thing has more objective value than something else.

The reality is that people value things differently and in the context of their own lives. They value something by what it means to them personally.

Each of us values things differently in terms of our own lives.

I could argue that this book is more intrinsically valuable than a comic book, but many would say that they like comic books better — and that is their right.

Capitalism is a market system where people deal with one another not by force but by trade.

Critics of the system seek to force their concept of value on the rest of us.

A capitalist society is one of trade and persuasion — not of force.

You seek to make the most of your life — to flourish. You judge every product, service, and idea by what you perceive to be its value to your life. That is the standard of value — you make a rational and emotional cost-benefit analysis.

So, even though you are sure that classical music has more intrinsic value than popular music, you may flip on a rock music station because you like it better.

You make choices about competing products, services, jobs, and ideas based on how they affect your life and how they make you feel.

You make mistakes (usually from not getting accurate or full information) and are misled sometimes.

If you find out that the product, service, job, or idea does not deliver as promised, you switch to something else.

Every so often, the concept of "comparable worth" is pushed by politicians and the media. Comparable worth tries to compare unrelated jobs, such as dentist, secretary, and truck driver, and then formulates a pay scale by political decree.

This is a case of people using the intrinsic worth argument, which is unworkable under a free-market system and takes away freedom.

It would set up centralized authorities to determine the proper pay for jobs based on intrinsic worth.

Essentially, intrinsic worth sets up someone's judgment of what something is worth to negate the market judgment and yours.

In a capitalist social system, the way to get people to try your product, service, or idea is through persuasion, discussion, advertising, etc.

Capitalism does not allow any group to force others to accept something.

Protection of individual rights is a central function of government, protecting you from such force.

Your freedom of speech in this country is linked to the freedom to trade values.

Economic and political freedom are part of the same fabric.

As I stated earlier, to advocate ideas, especially controversial ones, you need to access the materials necessary to spread your message. You need access to various media.

In a capitalist marketplace of freely competing interests, this is relatively easy to do. It is exceedingly difficult in a non-capitalist system, if not impossible unless you are part of the favored group of the moment.

Many critics of capitalism have tried to make the case that advertising creates artificial demand and lulls us into becoming consumers of goods we do not need.

What this argument does not recognize is that people can think and not just react. Do they always do so? After all, thinking takes work.

But most people learn very soon that advertising claims are not necessarily valid.

The product may not live up to its stated claims.

Therefore, most people have a healthy skepticism about advertising. (The same is true for political speech.)

What advertising does is let you know that a product is available and creates a favorable buying impulse that will disappear if the product does not live up to its promise.

Values in a capitalist system are based solely on your assessment of them in your life. If your judgment is not based on reason, you bear the consequences.

Now, it's time to consider the concepts of profit and loss.

PROFIT & LOSS

Photos by BP Miller on Unsplash

Capitalism is the freedom to gain profit or incur losses. You can make money or lose your shirt.

In either case, you learn and act accordingly on your next venture.

In life, there is no such thing as a sure thing — except objective reality.

In a capitalist system, participants (if they are smart) keep records to compare present results against past performance.

It is an always forward-looking system and growth oriented.

By comparing current results against previous results, you have an indication of how you are doing. You assess your current reality all the time.

If you have a bad year financially, it may have been caused by many factors, some outside your control.

In a capitalist system, you try not to make excuses for poor results — and aim for better results next time.

Your goal is profit, be it financial or intangible.

Profit is the result of successful deviation from the status quo.

Let us consider two scenarios.

You have risked your money, time, and energy on a new manufacturing process for your invention. With intelligent marketing and salesmanship, your new product is selling throughout the land.

It is a good product that people find useful. Your foresight, labor, and capital invested have paid off. You are taking in more money than you put in.

Your customers and your employees appreciate the value you created. You have created wealth by making a new or better product and marketed it successfully.

You take your profit and invest in more production capacity.

You also set up a research facility to come up with new and better products and ideas.

You keep your eyes open for new trends that could either help or hinder the industry you created.

Your profits continue because you take calculated risks and work hard to fulfill the demand for your product.

Let's consider another scenario. No one buys your invention. People don't like it or see a need for it.

What do you do?

You try new strategies and approaches. If this does not work and all else fails, you may have to take your losses.

Loss is the penalty for not satisfying demand, using obsolete methods, poor marketing, bad timing, hiring inefficient labor, customer apathy, or any combination of factors, many outside your control.

If you can identify what the problem is, you may be able to turn things around.

Capitalism gives you the freedom to fail as well as succeed.

The freedom to fail is also valuable. You learn from your failures and correct your mistakes.

Henry Ford failed three times when he started manufacturing automobiles. He succeeded on the fourth try.

Failure, adequately understood, teaches more eloquently than any sermon.

It tells you that you had better do more market research next time, or perhaps this is the wrong field to be in, or your timing was off.

The world is full of former "failures" who have found other ideas, products, or services to bring them success. Or have persisted until they succeeded.

Profit is justified by the time, money, energy, brainpower, foresight, planning, and hard work that goes into any success. You earned it!

Everyone acts to gain some form of profit. It can be in many forms — from money to a smile.

The bottom line is that someone earned it.

In a capitalist society, rewards accrue to those who earn them.

No one has a right to unearned rewards.

If someone chooses to help us, that is legitimate if we are in some way deserving of it and do not expect it as our right.

OFFENSE & DEFENSE

Photo by Mpho Mojapelo on Unsplash

As stated in this book's first sentence: Capitalism is an economic, social, and political system built upon individual initiative.

When groups of individuals join voluntarily to form businesses and corporations, it is individuals who choose whether to do so or not.

Capitalism is the economic system of the individual.

This section explores forces and ideas that either potentially destroy or help capitalism — government, enemies, and self-defense.

First, however, we need to go over some broad ideas that underlie our understanding or misunderstanding of capitalism.

This first idea is what I call the "economic pie syndrome." When someone says that they have finally got a piece of the pie, referring to economic success, this is part of the economic pie syndrome.

It's the belief that the total wealth of a country (or even the world) is static or limited. It is the belief that there is only one pie.

Advocates of Capitalism know that the pie is expanding, or new pies are baked all the time.

Those who have the limited view believe that one man's gain is another's loss. They think there are only a limited number of slices of an ever-diminishing pie. (Environmentalists take this mistaken view to its conclusion.)

The economic pie fallacy leads to a belief that one country's wealth is at the expense of developing nations. It means that they did not get their "piece" of the global pie or had their piece stolen by the rich countries.

Before we discuss this issue further, it is necessary to define "wealth."

Wealth is the value created via intelligence and labor. The earth's raw materials are of limited use until they are converted by brainpower and ability into something of value.

For instance, petroleum was sitting inside the earth for millennia but was worthless until the internal combustion engine.

To extract it from the earth required intelligence, foresight, capital, and labor. Then it had to be refined into a usable product.

Wealth is created. Was this wealth created at the expense of those who did not create it? Was it of any use to them in the first place?

Contrary to popular opinion, wealth is not a collective product of society or nature. Someone's mind, energy, and capital created it.

What about natural beauty? Isn't that a value? Of course. And it takes intelligence, foresight, labor, and capital to preserve and enhance it.

Consider another example, Edison's light bulb. Was it created at the expense of the rest of society, or was it a product that we all benefit from if we value light?

Interestingly, Edison (if he were alive today) would, most likely, have a hard time. He'd have to get past the inevitable anti-light bulb propaganda thrown at him from environments and other regulators.

Now back to the economic pie syndrome. Remember, this is the view that wealth is a limited commodity. It's a child-like view that all the wealth is in Uncle Scrooge's money bin—a static view of wealth that equates it with natural resources. (Full disclosure: I was an avid reader of Uncle Scrooges comic books when I was a kid.)

Resources are of limited value until uses are found for them, and they are converted into products. The capitalist outlook of wealth is the opposite of the economic pie syndrome.

Wealth is not limited but created by human ability, and intelligence applied to the problems of life. Raw materials are "raw" until shaped toward a purpose.

The major battle of ideas going on in the world today results from the conflict between two ideas.

The first idea is that society is the most important and crucial agency in the world. So, we all must be required to work together for society's goals.

The other idea is that the individual is the essential agent in the world and must be free to think, plan, and take actions based on rational self-interest.

It's collectivism vs. individualism.

One is the collective, beehive, or anthill approach to humanity, and the other is an individual human being approach.

Those with a collective mentality want to force their collective goals on the rest of us.

They hate capitalism because it is a system that works on individual self-interest and freedom of choice.

In the chapter on enemies, we will take a deeper dive into this philosophy and other strains in more detail.

Capitalism is best understood from the individual perspective and not the collective.

Let us now spend time on the critical subject of government as it relates to capitalism.

GOVERNMENT

Photo by Darren Halstead on Unsplash

The government in a capitalist or free society is necessary but potentially dangerous.

It is necessary because a capitalist society needs a stable base of objective law to lay the ground rules for behavior and facilitate the free exchange of goods, services, and ideas.

Such objective law allows a capitalist system to thrive. It does this by protecting individual rights.

Yet, government is dangerous because the history of the world is strewn with victims of government abuse.

Government is like a powerful machine because it has the legal monopoly of force. It must not be left untended or allowed to get into unscrupulous hands.

When Jefferson wrote the Declaration of Independence, it was not meant to stand alone. To establish the ideals of that document, a Constitution was necessary. It created the machinery of freedom. Legitimate government is the machinery of freedom.

The basis of government is the protection of individual rights.

Rights are conditions necessary for pursuing the course of our lives, such as the freedom to think, to write, to act, and to associate.

As John Locke stated hundreds of years ago, the law's purpose is not to limit our freedom but to increase it.

Everyone's right to pursue his own life's interest is sacred under a capitalist system. The *initiation* of force by any person, group, or government is illegal because it violates this right.

Under a capitalist society, the government is an umpire, not a general manager (as it's become in a mixed economy). In a collectivist society, government becomes a vampire.

The essential functions of government are the police, the courts, and the armed forces. They are tools to protect individual rights and not agents for violating rights.

To see what can happen without a functioning government or a weak government, look at the numerous examples throughout modern history.

A weak government is powerless to control the armed gangs that always are shooting at each other and killing innocent civilians. It is impossible under these circumstances to carry on everyday life.

A government has the legal monopoly on using force (*to retali-*

ate) to protect individual rights.

We as individuals have the right to protect ourselves, especially if the government is not doing the job. But the government has the sole authority over the retaliatory use of force.

If everyone could retaliate for every wrong done to them, there would be chaos everywhere. (Look at the criminal gangs of Chicago and other major cities as an example of what can happen.)

Yet when the government is not doing its job of protecting individual rights, law-abiding individuals are forced to defend themselves as best they can.

The government ensures that we can carry on the affairs of our lives in relative safety. It also settles civil disputes (Torts).

In recent times, the government has taken on new roles that take away its power to carry out its legitimate functions.

Some of the new roles it has taken on are the welfare state and regulating economic activity (the mixed economy).

The modern welfare state and the mixed economy would take volumes to describe. The harm it does daily is incalculable. It enters the economic life of individual action and starts interfering with exchanging goods, services, and ideas in myriad and subtle ways.

The welfare state is one of the sources of the economic pie syndrome. It makes the limited benefits a cause for petty squabbling and jealousy.

Look how people look with disdain upon immigrants as extra mouths to feed. This is economic pie thinking that overlooks individuals.

The government in a mixed economy and welfare state has combined politics and economics — a deadly and dangerous combination.

Separation of religion and politics is vital to individual freedom. So is the separation of economics and politics.

When economic decisions are a matter of political control or interference, our freedom of action, which is the basis of capitalism, is severely limited.

Most, if not all, of our economic crises and monopolies, were caused by government interference into the economy — granting special favors to the political in-group of the moment and penalizing those not politically connected.

Capitalism is, first and foremost, the separation of economics and politics. So-called "state capitalism" is a contradiction in terms.

Government interference into the economy at any and every level dilutes capitalism, so it becomes relatively unrecognizable.

The welfare state is a gradual process of decay. It was allegedly to help people but instead encourages dependence on government *benefits* — which are simply the funds confiscated from individuals through taxation and deficit spending.

The only cure for this trend is the full restoration of Laissez-faire capitalism, which is real capitalism.

If the government can control or severely prescribe your actions, then it can control your mind. Thoughts without the possibility of action are fruitless.

The modern advocates of welfare, the mixed-economy, and outright socialism, want to wrap us in flannel and treat us as children who cannot think or act for themselves and must obey government masters.

We will now look at the true nature of our enemies and why they hate capitalism.

WHAT MOTIVATES THE ENEMIES OF CAPITALISM?

Photo by Andre Hunter on Unsplash

First and foremost, the enemies of capitalism hate it because it works so well.

They are reactionaries — reacting against capitalism.

Capitalism focuses on this life and this world.

It is successful, it works, and people can thrive under it.

Of course, enemies of capitalism will phrase their hatred of capitalism's success in terms of concern for the poor and unsuccessful, or the alleged harm it does to the environment.

Capitalism is hated because it works. As Ayn Rand wrote about our enemies: they hate the good for being "the good." Jealousy and envy further fuel anti-capitalism.

A critic made an interesting comment about capitalism as he was interviewed on television quite some time ago. He said that capitalism was "irrational" because it "spilled surpluses all over the place." He was not concerned that it didn't work but that it worked too well.

Yes, capitalism is as "irrational" as nature itself. Capitalism utilizes nature's principles of abundance.

The enemies and critics of capitalism hate it for much more profound and fundamental reasons. An advocate of capitalism must know what motivates our enemies.

The real issue is philosophical.

To advocates of any variant of collectivism, the essence of right action is altruistic intention. If you do something for an allegedly "altruistic" reason — meaning not for yourself but for others — then the action is good, regardless of the means or the consequences.

An altruistic motive is all-important to a collectivist, whether they call themselves environmentalists, socialists, communists, terrorists, fascists, or any variant of the collective mentality, including religious fanatics. Right action is allegedly done for the good of "the people" or some vengeful god.

They are believers in the concept I mentioned earlier — intrinsic value. They believe that some things are good regardless of their consequences. And therefore, if it is necessary to deprive some people of their freedom, property, or even life, then so be it.

45

Another strain of this is the belief that if the desired result is "good," then the means used do not matter. In other words, the ends justify the means.

If you want to know why there are so many apologists for repressive societies, this is why: To them, "the good," whatever it may be, can and perhaps must be achieved by force.

The enemies of capitalism view life from a collective frame of reference. They view the individual as expendable, if necessary.

They view our concepts of freedom and liberty as bourgeois sentimentality — except for themselves.

They reject the notion that individuals should be free to choose their purposes in life and act accordingly — which is the essence of capitalism.

It all goes back to their philosophical roots.

To them, the action is pure if it is altruistic and selfless.

When one acts in self-interest, it is suspect and not morally significant, no matter that the results are beneficial.

A benefit destroys the moral value of an action. It must be selfless, even if a sea of blood may result.

Their rhetoric proclaims concern for the poor and less fortunate, but their real concern is their lust for power. The compulsion to control is at the heart of all enemies of capitalism.

Power lust is alive and well. It thrives on envy and the hatred of the successful for being successful. And capitalism is the most successful social system the world has ever seen.

Capitalism is a system built on rational selfishness, i.e., pursuing your own life without violating others' rights.

It is a system that recognizes and codifies the fact that you own your own life.

Capitalism's enemies want to rule those inferior beings, grappling with life every day in their "selfish" pursuit of success and happiness.

If this sounds irrational, it is. The enemies of capitalism hate the independent, rational, self-interested mind, anchored to reality. The businessman and businesswoman have come to symbolize this rational selfishness that they despise.

Although it may sound contradictory, our enemies, although being irrational, are also philosophical rationalists. In this sense, rationalism is the belief and practice that one can reason without reference to reality. One creates one's own reality.

An idea to a rationalist may not have any basis in reality and may even contradict it. But this does not stop a rationalist.

They ignore reality and prove their case using logical arguments build on illogical, unreal, and untrue premises.

Many have blamed logic, but logic is only valid if it is based on truth. It is a tool and, as with all tools, can be used for good or evil.

To such "rationalists," their idea of the good supersedes everything, even the real world. They argue their case based on false premises.

Then, it allows them to ignore capitalism's record and explain why a socialist or religious utopia will liberate humanity.

What it does is liberate humankind from life, liberty, and the pursuit of happiness.

What stands in the way of their impossible pipe dreams is the middle class, capitalist consumer lifestyle, and world trade.

Those in the middle class believe in the system, thrive on it, and make it work.

All collectivists, including modern-day terrorists, want to destroy the middle class and middle-class life. They want to terror-ize and scare the middle class.

Aristotle remarked that the middle class is the stable class that makes for a stable society. A stable society stands in the way of our enemy's dream of conquest and control.

Therefore, their goal is to disrupt middle-class life throughout the world with acts of sowing confusion, scare tactics, subver-sion, and even terrorism.

Their ideas are child-like fantasies of wealth without effort and happiness without achievement.

Modern life is too complicated for them. For some, it would be more fun to loot and live off the carcass of Western Civilization.

Environmentalism, socialism, communism, and fascism are re-actions against the modern world — against technology, pro-gress, growth, and worldly happiness.

What about the more moderate socialists (or religionists) who seem to value modern civilization? Their underlying motives may be the same, but they seem to preach reasonableness and moderation.

They plan to control the economy by political action, thus negat-ing freedom of choice — a slow poisoning, leading eventually to destruction and death.

They want society, the nation, the state, and the community to decide economic issues.

They house their arguments as a battle against "inequality of wealth," calling for democratic control of the economy, which means democratic control of individuals, their property, and their mind.

The essence of property is the right of disposal and decision. By taking away individuals and businesses' right to decide how to use and dispose of their property, socialists, environmentalists, and collectivists will have achieved the dream of all powerlusters to control human beings effectively.

Socialists (and environmentalists) want to plan how to use "societies" (or "nature's") resources. They want to control and decide how individuals use their wealth and property.

This collectivist mentality is at the root of all their misconceptions and deceptions about capitalism.

They have neat, organized plans for our unpredictable economy.

The economy is the sum of our actions when we get out of bed in the morning—across the world.

They want to plan and control our actions and lives while spending our money to do it and expecting our moral sanction.

Their attack on capitalism is an attack on our consumer and produce society. They don't like the unequal results of people freely choosing how to spend their time and their lives.

Capitalism is a system of equal opportunity and possibility to pursue one's dreams.

Enemies of capitalism want equal results. The only way to get equal results is to hold down anyone who rises too far and keep everyone on the same level. Therefore, they are always harping against "the rich." They want to conjure up envy among the less informed.

Enemies of capitalism hate the successful for being successful. They hate luxuries for being luxuries. They hate anyone who values their own life enough to say, "hands off."

Collectivists cannot tolerate those who are self-assured and unashamed of their success.

All enemies of capitalism have a puritanical and dogmatic streak in them that sees capitalism as sinful self-indulgence.

We need to remember that the enemies of capitalism allegedly want to take away the pain from life but instead take away the pleasure.

Human pleasure is what they cannot stand, especially pleasure that is freely chosen by individuals. They cannot tolerate rational, self-interested pleasure.

They are, at heart, worshipers of pain and death. And that is what they offer the world.

So, how do we defend ourselves from these life haters and potential destroyers? Read on.

SELF-DEFENSE

Photo by Chris Chow on Unsplash

Our first defense against the anti-capitalist rhetoric that our enemies throw at us is to think clearly and think for ourselves.

Think in terms of the individual and beware of the collective, macro-economic thinking that is prevalent today.

When someone says "society should do something about it" or that "we owe society" something, your ears should perk up, and you should be ready to defend your freedom.

Society is composed of individuals. Individuals are the central players in life. The individual can change the course of the world on a small scale or a large one.

Socialists try to use the government to pass laws to force individuals to think and do things in a certain way.

Destroying initiative destroys progress.

The price of liberty is philosophical vigilance, which means knowing your case right down to its basic principles.

Our enemies, although irrational, are nonetheless *consistent*. We must be consistent if we are to win the battle for our lives, liberty, and happiness.

Those who are consistent and do not back down from philosophical confrontation can fight and win this battle.

When our enemies call for more government control of our lives — think of the company town.

In our history, some companies have made many attempts, such as the Pullman Company, to set up whole cities owned and operated by the company. Their intentions were usually honorable.

You rented a company house, bought groceries in a company store. Your children went to company-provided schools. You got married in a company-built church. You were buried in a company cemetery.

For some, it could be a cradle to grave company town.

The downside to all this was that the company began to tell you how to live your life.

If you wanted to go elsewhere, however, there was no one to stop you. The borders were not surrounded by barbed wire.

Think for a minute about what the collectivists want to do. They want to make the whole country into a vast company town.

But this time, there is no place else to go, except leaving the country *if they let you.*

The former Soviet Union and current North Korea and Cuba are such company town countries. However, the "Company" is an all-powerful government — ready, willing, and able to force its citizens to comply with its dictates.

People are allegedly taken care of but at a terrible price — their freedom.

If you disagreed under such a system, how could you finance your cause?

The company/country owns everything, including newspapers and the YMCA Hall.

If you speak out, you could get fired — and where else can you work when the government owns everything and is the sole employer?
Or they could arrest you and lock you up forever.

To defend your freedom, do not apologize for your success or your position in life.

Enemies of Capitalism use guilt as a coercive tool. If they can make you feel guilty for your success, they can control you for life.

Lately, they have pushed forward the racist idea of "white privilege" in a blatant attempt to make one feel guilty for their race (if one happens to be white).

Call it for what it is — racism! Such racism is a total rejection of individualism and the individual, no matter what one's race.

Learn to defend your principles when attacked.

Do not remain silent. If you do not know how to argue your case, you can state that you disagree with the speaker. By doing so, you may also give others the courage to speak up.

Learn to be truly selfish. To be genuinely selfish means viewing your life as your province — your precious commodity. Don't waste. It is all you have.

To be selfish means that you want to put only the best food into your body and not cheap garbage.

Plan also to put the best ideas into your head.

To be selfish means that you want the best for yourself and your family and are willing to work hard for it.

This selfishness is long-term thinking that wants happiness and not suffering to be the outcome of your life.

A rational philosophy can give you a blueprint for living such a life. I highly recommend Ayn Rand's philosophy of Objectivism. See suggested readings at the end of this book.

There are three tests that you can use when analyzing any idea or argument you may hear or read:

#1) Is this a collective perspective or an individual perspective?

In other words, is this a view that considers us as mere components of a collective *or* as active agents of change and unique individuals?

When you hear statements about society's obligation or the distribution of resources, translate this into individual terms such as personal responsibility, buying, selling, and producing goods.

#2) Ask if force is necessary to implement a policy?

When people advocate such things as "Medicare for all" or compulsory national service, they seldom mention the coercive force needed to implement these policies.

 In the case of compulsory national service (or the draft), these will be implemented by forcing young men and women to give up their freedom, bodies, and possibly, lives.

#3) (This test is from Ayn Rand.) **Ask yourself: If I were to accept**

this statement as true, what would follow?

Or what would be the logical outcome if such a view were implemented or made real? Or what is the final goal?

If someone says, for instance, "children should be seen and not heard," what might follow? Children would grow up unable to express a viewpoint.

Or "One man's gain is another man's loss" would mean that every time you put a piece of food in your stomach, you are robbing it from those who do not have food. It's the economic pie scenario that I wrote about earlier.

When arguing your case, make sure you anchor your arguments to reality. Do not get caught up in the rationalist attempt to argue without reference to the facts.

Above all, you must fight *for* capitalism, not just against its enemies.

Have a good defense, of course, but a good offense is the best defense. Know your case and do not apologize for success and happiness and what makes it possible — capitalism and the individual human creativity it releases.

But remember, this is just the beginning of gaining newfound knowledge and respect for capitalism.

"Capitalism was the only system in history where wealth was not acquired by looting, but by production, not by force, but by trade, the only system that stood for man's right to his own mind, to his work, to his life, to his happiness, to himself." — Ayn Rand

AFTERWORD

Ayn Rand was a great defender and advocate of capitalism. I urge you to read her novels and non-fiction. Her most insightful and exciting story about the motive power of Capitalism was *Atlas Shrugged*.

Rand will give you the intellectual ammunition and moral certainty needed to become an unequivocal advocate of capitalism, as well as benefit from its principles. She was the main inspiration for the research I put into this book.

Another influential defender and advocate of Capitalism was Ludwig von Mises. His *Human Action* is the closest book to a modern economic bible you will find.

Closely behind von Mises is George Reisman with his magisterial book *Capitalism: A Treatise on Economics*.

Finally, the classic economic work that began it all is *The Wealth of Nations* by Adam Smith.

The following Bibliography offers more.

BIBLIOGRAPHY

As stated in my preface to this book, I spent much time and effort studying everything that could help me and my potential readers understand and appreciate capitalism better and thus realize why capitalism always beats socialism.

Here are some of the books that helped me and might help you understand capitalism and socialism better. Some may be out-of-print but may still be available from Amazon or other book dealers. Some are available on Kindle, eBook, or audio editions.

Capitalism by Arthur Seldon

Capitalism: The Unknown Ideal by Ayn Rand

Comparative Economic Systems by William N. Loucks

Economic Development: Past and Present by Richard T. Gill

Economics in One Lesson by Henry Hazlitt

Essentials of Economics by Faustino Ballvé

For the New Intellectual by Ayn Rand

Human Action by Ludwig von Mises

Ideologies and Modern Politics by Christenson, Engel, Jacobs, Rejai, and Waltzer - 2nd edition

Marx and the Marxists: The Ambiguous Legacy by Sidney Hook

Objectivism: The Philosophy of Ayn Rand by Leonard Peikoff

Principles of Political Economy by John Stuart Mill and Jonathan

Riley (editor)

Prophet of Progress: selections from the speeches of Charles F. Kettering

Recapturing the Spirit of Enterprise by George Gilder (This is an updated edition of the one I first used.)

The Anti-Capitalist Mentality by Ludwig von Mises

The Economy of Cities by Jane Jacobs

The God of the Machine by Isabel Patterson

The Next Economy by Paul Hawken

The Roots of Capitalism by John Chamberlain

The Theory of Economic Progress by C. E. Ayres

The Triumph of American Capitalism by Louis M. Hacker

Time Will Run Back a novel by Henry Hazlitt

University Economics by Alchian Armen Albert (Author), William R. Allen (Author) Books by This Author

OTHER BOOKS BY KEN WEST

Get What You Want

A short, practical workbook designed to guide anyone to achieve his or her dreams and happiness. How? By navigating the reader through a logical, 7-step series of powerful, probing questions and writing down the workbook's answers.

Get What You Want is a book that will help you achieve your goals by staying true to yourself. It's especially beneficial to those at the crossroads of life, trying to find a direction that makes sense.

Editor's note: Ken's original book, *Get What You Want*, was re-published on the CreateSpace Publishing Platform in 2017 with the updated title, *Achieve Your Purpose*. It's the same great content as the original book (which is also still available on Amazon).

Ken's Books Coming Soon

Life Zones: They are the 31 areas of your life that help boost your productivity, renewal, and sense of well-being, outlined, and discussed.

Ego's Journey: This is the story of how an ego got warped and stunted — and how it got healthy.

Motivation and Self-Discipline: A practical toolbox for getting your most important goals achieved.

ABOUT THE AUTHOR

Ken describes his writing (and speaking) mission this way:

"How can you accelerate your passion, purpose, and talents? That's my focus."

"I also write about political and social issues, especially how to preserve, protect, and defend freedom."

Ken is a past President of the New England Chapter of the National Speakers Association and the Association of Objectivist Businessmen.

He was the Editor-in-Chief of *AOB News*, the association's monthly journal.

Currently, Ken is the Editor of the weekly online publication, the *Matrix Gazette*.

He is also the Publishing and Social Media Manager for a sales training and management consulting firm.

Ken divides his time between Southwest Florida and New England.

He can be reached via email at

KenWest@BetterGripMedia.com

"The essence of Capitalism is the empowerment of private, productive purpose. *You* decide your purpose, no one else."

— Ken West